AND THE SONG GOES ON...

OLDER ADULTS IN MUSIC MINISTRY

Linda B. Hansen
with Betsy Pittard Styles, Consultant

Abingdon Press
Nashville

AND THE SONG GOES ON. . .
Older Adults in Music Ministry

Copyright © 1995 by Abingdon Press

This book is printed on acid-free, recycled paper.

ISBN 0-687-01147-7

95 96 97 98 99 00 01 02 03 04 — 10 9 8 7 6 5 4 3 2 1

MANUFACTURED IN THE UNITED STATES OF AMERICA

AND THE SONG
GOES ON...

For my husband, Bob,
and children, Katie, Charlotte, and Jessica,
who allow me the gift of time
to pursue God's call,
and for my mother, Ann,
who supports me in many beautiful ways.

Contents

Preface

This book has been written for the person who has little or no formal training or experience in organizing a new choir but who has been called to begin an older adult music ministry. I hope that it will give you a clear and concise plan for beginning a new choir for older adults.

This book is arranged in chapters with subsections to help you easily find the information you need. Related worship resources are listed in the back with information on how to obtain permission to use copyrighted materials.

Working with older adults can be one of the most rewarding and challenging experiences you will ever discover. It is also an adventure! The books and other publications listed in the bibliography will be the starting point for additional readings, resources, and information.

Let the adventure begin!

Linda B. Hansen

Chapter One
Getting to Know Older Adults

Who is the older adult? By what guidelines do we determine exactly when a person reaches the older adult stage of life? Pension systems, some businesses, and various agencies have viewed this stage as beginning at retirement. However, this stage of life is not so much an exact age as it is the way each individual views his or her life.

When you begin to look at the older adult years, you will see that it is difficult to label absolutely any part of this group chronologically. A number of writers have tried to divide this stage into clearly defined groups according to age, such as "younger" old (55–74), "middle" old (75–85) and "old" old (86 and beyond). Even gerontologists do not agree on chronological categorization. Speaking from my own experience, I simply cannot define a total group in terms of their age.

I have known a number of older adults, eighty years of age or older, whom I would describe as being "younger" old adults, and I have also known some adults in their sixties whom I would describe as being "middle" old to "old" old. It really depends on how the older adult views himself or herself and how active and responsive he or she is in the day-to-day art of living. In fact, the older adult tends to move in and out of the various stages. All older adults are not alike; it is not a homogeneous group but rather a group of individuals with many experiences.

Another method used for describing the stages of life divides life into quarters. The first quarter is 1 through 25; the second, 26 through 50; the third quarter, 51 through 75; and the fourth quarter, 76 through 100. The older adult quarters are the third and fourth. Perhaps this method is a better one to use, although we should consider adding a fifth quarter for those who are now living well beyond one hundred years. This method points to another important reason for having intentional older adult ministries within the church. The older adult years involve multi-quarters. Most of us will live longer in the older adult quarters than in other stages of life.

Most of us are probably guilty to one degree or another of having stereotypes concerning older adults. One Christmas a few years ago, I was standing in the sanctuary talking with one of my friends who had just celebrated a birthday. When I asked if she would mind telling me how old she was, this active, lovely lady replied, "Why, I'm ninety-four and proud of every year!"

I could not keep from exclaiming that she certainly didn't look ninety-four. My friend looked me straight in the eye and said, "Honey, maybe you need to know that this is what ninety-four looks like!" The time has come for all of us to put away the stereotypes and see older adults as they really are.

If you look at the local church congregation, you will see that this particular group is on the increase. There is a wealth of information pointing to the fact that the number of older adults in the congregation is growing. While this group is experiencing rapid growth, it is also too often one of the most overlooked. Consider for a moment, the usual staffing of a local church. After the basic staff of pastor, secretary, and director of program or music is in place, the next position most often added is that of youth minister or director. Funding is usually readily available for youth ministry and great emphasis is rightly placed on this particular group. After all, the youth will be the next generation of supporting church members. But does not the church also have a basic responsibility to those persons known as older adults?

The older adult helped to plant and build each local church. The older adult has helped the church to be a vital part of the community. If you consider the number of years the older adults have been members of the congregation, you begin to see that they have given more of themselves, their resources, and their means to the work of the church than any other group in the church today.

Consider, too, that when they are not visiting family members, traveling, providing care for family members, or perhaps dealing with a personal illness, older adults are some of the most faithful attendants of local church activities and worship. The older adult typically does not want to sit and remember what he or she did in the past but rather seeks new ways to be involved in the life of the church. Changes in family responsibilities or paid work roles create opportunities to renew former activities and perhaps to participate in new activities or programs. The older adult may be looking for a way in which to be a vital part of ministry. Being involved in the ministry of music can be an exciting way for an individual to serve his or her church.

An older adult ministry can help older adults see themselves as important—those God loves, those God can use, those appreciated by their peers, those honored by their subordinates and those accepted and viewed with pride.

Why a ministry to older adults? Because the older adults in your church are saying:

> I want to be a friend, to be loved, to love.
> I want to be me.
> I want to do something.
> I want to go somewhere.
> I want to be recognized.
> I want to be growing.
> I want to be appreciated.
> I want to be serving.
> I want to be worshiping.

> I want to be clean, combed, clothed.
> I want to be comforted.
> I want to be ready.[1]

As you then consider the possibility of forming an older adult choir, there are a few basic questions you will need to answer. First, where are the older adults in your church or community? Most churches have one or more Sunday school classes composed of people who fit this classification. Some churches may also have an organized group, such as United Methodist Men or Women, or a club that meets on a regular basis. Older adults can also be found through eat-and-meet or travel groups in the church or in community centers sponsored by AARP, Parks and Recreation Golden Agers, or Shepherd's Centers, to name just a few. Attend some of these meetings to get to know the older adults and let them become acquainted with you.

As you begin to visit some of these groups, listen to the way these older adults refer to themselves. "Senior Saints," "Go Getters," "Service Club," and "Spice of Life" are just a few names of groups I have known and served. Older adults can have beautiful and positive self-images. Observe the way the older adults interact. You will find persons excited about life and enthusiastic about the avenues of service open to them. You will also find people who, at times, are less than happy, who may have experienced illness or loss of loved ones. Older adults are like every other age group. You will find a variety of personalities and abilities.

The next question to ask yourself is whether the older adults are interested in forming a choir. You might consider volunteering to lead some informal singing following a meal or program. If hymnals or songbooks are available, pass them out

1. J. Stanley Rendahl, *Working with Older Adults* (Berkley, Calif.: Harvest Publications, 1984), 14.

and lead songs that the group chooses. Encourage the members of the group to help select some of the songs. These may be old favorites or new ones. Look at the texts of the songs that are selected. Is there a theme that recurs, or is there a style of hymn that seems to be a favorite? This information will help you prepare for the next time you meet with this group.

Listen and watch the group as they sing. If they seem to enjoy singing together, the next time you attend one of their meetings come prepared with a simple anthem to pass out after they have sung a few hymns or choruses. Encourage them to watch you as you direct the song. Suggest that they stand or sit together as a choir just to see how the song sounds.

If you feel that there is an interest in forming a choir, you might want to try a short-term, limited vocal project to motivate even more interest. One success can generate interest in expanding the opportunity to formally organize a choir.

I learned early in my work with older adults not to be afraid of texts that use words like "old," "death," "dying," or "feeble." When the 1989 *United Methodist Hymnal* was being prepared, some of the proposed songs and samples of the psalter were introduced to many local congregations in a little book called *The Sampler.*

Having been invited to a gathering of the Service Club, a club of older adults in a local church, I decided to introduce them to the new hymnal through using *The Sampler.* One of the songs in this book was the old favorite "Stand By Me" by Charles Albert Tindley. Not wanting to offend any of my older singers, I elected not to sing the last verse, "When I'm growing old and feeble, stand by me." As we finished singing the first four verses, and before I could announce the next song, a woman with snow-white hair said, "I think we need to sing that last verse, too." The whole group agreed with her.

I had just learned an important lesson. Older adults know how old they are and how long they have lived. They know that while the future may hold some uncertainties, they can face it bravely, knowing that they are not alone. They seek to affirm their rightful place in many ways, including through music. Texts can be uplifting, affirming, and empowering. And certain texts, like the one just mentioned can have a powerful message when sung by a group of older adults. My friend in the Service Club had been right. They did need to sing that particular text, but I also needed to hear it.

Older adults have a message that they need to share and we all need to hear. The older adults in your congregation may decide that a choir is one way to offer this message.

Chapter Two
Starting the Older Adult Choir

Place

O nce you have decided that there is an interest in forming a choir even for a short-term or limited project, the
first order of business is to find a meeting place. This
place should be in a familiar area and accessible to all the
members of the choir. If you have gotten to know the people
who will be part of this new choir you may be aware of certain
physical limitations. If not, then you will need to talk with a
person who works with the older adults or has a close association with them to determine if there are any special needs to
be considered.

You would not want to choose a site on a second or third
floor, for example, if there will be choir members who do not
climb stairs easily, unless there is a ramp or elevator available
to them. Some very active older adults have had joint or hip
replacement, which can make them less certain about climbing
flights of stairs on a regular basis. You may also learn that one
or more individuals in a wheelchair or those who walk with the
aid of a walker may not be able to participate if the site is not
accessible.

The room selected should be large enough for the group to
gather comfortably and to accommodate a piano. Avoid practicing in your sanctuary. Singing in a new choir can be intimi-
dating. One of the things that can affect an older adult is a fear

of failure (this will be discussed later). Your new choir members may not sing as confidently as they did when you met with them following a dinner meeting in a smaller room. They may even sing more softly and in a large room, such as a sanctuary, the sound will be lost. You want this experience to be positive in every way, with a level of success felt by every person present. It is important that the size of the room not overwhelm the novice choir member.

Lighting/Comfort

Lighting in a particular room is also a consideration. You need light that is bright but not glaring. You also need a room arrangement that will enable the singer to read the music without a shadow falling across the page from the singer's head or another person or object. Overhead lighting is excellent, but if you meet in a room that uses lamps, make sure the wattage is at least seventy-five. If you have three lamps in a medium-sized room, each with a forty-watt light bulb, you would still not have enough light to make the music easy to read for all of your choir members.

If you have meetings during the day, shades and blinds against reflection glare experienced by persons with cataracts would be helpful. While security lighting for a nighttime meeting is a necessity, glaring spotlights are another problem.

One characteristic of a room that you are sure to hear about from your choir (especially if there is a problem) is the temperature! You will not be able to please everyone at all times, but as you select the room for your choir, try to find one in which you can control the temperature and the flow of air. If this is not possible, make sure your choir members know to bring sweaters in case it is too cool or to dress in layers that can be removed if it gets a little too warm.

If your choir meets at night, it is important that the church

or meeting place have a well-lighted parking lot. The entryways into and out of the building also need to be carefully
lighted. A handrail at the entryways would also give choir
members a safer access. Older adults have difficulty in moving
from one lighted area to a differently lighted area because
their eyes do not adjust to the difference as easily as they once
did. This is one reason why older adults are sometimes reluc-
tant to come to night meetings.

Music

The printing style of the music you select is a special consideration. Everyone has different vision needs, but attention
to some basic elements will ensure that the music is readable
for most.

Small print can be hard to read. If you are purchasing new
octavos, be sure the print is not small and that it is in a dark
color (black is the most accepted). If you are going to be using
a hymnal, the print should be acceptable, and if you are using
a soft-cover songbook make sure that the print is easy to read.
The color of the printed page is also important. A light-colored
page (white or off-white) with clear dark print is best.

You may find that one or more of your choir members
needs a large-print score. I once had a person in my chancel
choir who was legally blind. She was an excellent musician but
needed a very large score. I learned that if I contacted the publisher of the anthem we were using, I usually could obtain permission to enlarge the score for this person. Occasionally I had
to pay a one-time fee to do this (no more than $10.00), but
often, after explaining that I had purchased enough copies of a
piece for each choir member (including the one who needed
the enlarged score), I would be given permission to make the
copy needed at no cost to me.

Copying is illegal, but publishers are not unaware of cer-

tain needs in choirs and in my experience have been very helpful in dealing with a particular problem. Some scores are now
available in large print. In your local Christian music store you
should be able to find a few cantatas or octavos available in
the larger print. If not, *ask* for them. Ask the manager of the
store and then take the time to write to the publisher of the
piece in which you are interested. The more we ask for certain
styles of print, the more publishers are aware of the need for
this kind of music.

If you use separate octavos or several different collections,
your choir members will need a way to store their individual
sets of music. A choral folio, available from choral supply
stores, or a large accordion pleated folder, purchased at an
office supply store, will serve this purpose. In addition to storage folders you will need performance folders. Older adults
know how a choir should look during a worship service or performance, and they will want to look just as polished.

A way to combine a storage folder with a performance
folder is to use a black two- or three-ring folder (similar to a
handbell folder but smaller) that holds all of your octavos. You
will need to punch holes in each piece of music to fit the style
of notebook. This method offers an advantage for the older
adult choir is that you can arrange the octavos in the same
order in each book, simplifying the process of locating the
pieces. Also, since the octavos are held in place by the rings,
lost pages or dropped music is less of a concern.

If you are really organized, you can even purchase some
restickable tabs or flags in various colors (available at office
supply stores) to stick on each octavo. Then during rehearsal
you simply announce the name of the next piece and the color
of the flag where the piece is located. Just remember not to
overload the notebook or your choir member may not be able
to hold it!

Either number each folder or write the name of each choir

member on his or her folder. This will enable the singer to identify his or her own music. Provide a chart or notebook so that choir members may check out their music to rehearse at home.

Chairs/Arrangement

Give thought to the type of chairs you will use for your choir. Most churches have folding chairs available for use by various groups. If these are what you must use, be sure that they will not slip when choir members sit down or get up. Most folding chairs start off with rubber tips on the legs, but through years of use these can deteriorate or fall off. New rubber tips can be purchased at a variety of stores that sell this type of chair. If the floor in the practice area is carpeted, the folding chair should not slip.

Straight-backed, lightly padded chairs, with narrow armrests, if possible, are preferable. They are more comfortable and encourage better posture. Armrests enable the older adult who has a problem getting up to use his or her hands to assist in getting out of the chair.

Arrange the chairs to provide enough room between the rows so that choir members do not feel as though they are climbing over one another to get to a seat. Give each member a little room on either side, enough for purses or books to be put on the floor and out of the way of anyone who needs to walk past. If you are using folding chairs or some other chair that does not have arm rests, you may discover that there is a member who needs an empty chair beside him or her for help in getting up.

The room where you meet may be used by other groups. If there are tables in the room that are used for dinners or other meetings, make sure that they are not in the way of your chair arrangement. Tables can be moved against the walls and provide a place for coats, music, or coffee and refreshments.

Time

When it comes to establishing a rehearsal time, be sure to consult directly with the participants (in an organizational meeting or after one of their regularly scheduled meetings), or develop a registration form, similar to the one below, that will provide the information you need to determine the best time for all members to meet.

REGISTRATION FORM

Name _____

Address _____

City _____ State _____ Zip _____

Phone (daytime) _____ (evening) _____

What is your birthday? (month, day) _____

Does most of your family live in your town? _____

Do you drive? _____ Could you carpool? _____

Can you meet during the day? _____ or evening? _____

What are your interests? (hobbies, children, grandchildren, occupation, interests). Use the back if necessary.

_____

_____

_____

A registration form similar to the one shown will tell you a great deal about your new singers. Also, you will be able to determine if the majority want a daytime or evening rehearsal.

If a daytime rehearsal is requested, try to schedule it during the midmorning hours or early afternoon. Older adults lead very full and busy lives. By scheduling a midmorning rehearsal, you will leave the main portion of the morning for their other activities, such as errands, appointments, and so on. But also remember that a morning rehearsal may be difficult for the arthritic person.

If an evening rehearsal is preferred, try to schedule it just after the dinner hour. Most older adults, and some middle-aged or younger adults, do not like to be out late at night, especially if they will be driving alone. If you have access to a church van or bus, see if any in your group would like to have a pickup service made available. This might be a way to involve persons outside of the choir in this new endeavor.

Should you decide that a van or bus pickup is going to be needed, you will need to find two persons to travel on the bus or van. One will drive the vehicle, and the other will go to the door to escort each person to the bus. As the church vehicle takes the singers home after rehearsal, the person who escorts the singer to the door will take the time to make sure the choir member is safely inside before leaving. An extra step can be added to church vans to help the older adult in getting in and out of the vehicle. If a step cannot be added, a portable step-stool should be kept in the van.

From the registration forms you also will be able to determine if there are times when a large number of choir members will be gone. If a choir members responds that his or her family does not live in the same town, this will be an indication that at holidays this member may be with family and not at the regular rehearsals. It could also mean that the family would be at the choir member's home for a family holiday and the singer would not be able to come to the rehearsal. You will begin to learn whether you need to suspend rehearsals over short periods of time during holiday seasons.

If any choir members check that they enjoy traveling, try to find out if this travel involves long periods of a particular season. From this information you will be able to determine if there are times during the year when it would not be feasible to hold regular rehearsals.

Publicity

Once these initial decisions have been made, you can begin to publicize your new choir opportunity. You can put brief, well-worded announcements in your church newsletter, make an announcement at the beginning of a Sunday school class, or perhaps go back to the meeting where you first met these older adults and address the whole group. These are some of the easier ways to get the word out about your new group, but if you have the time you can get really creative.

If there is a bulletin board that you can use for a few weeks prior to the first organized meeting, fill it with cutouts of older adults engaged in all kinds of activities. You can use a wide variety of old magazines and catalogues to find these pictures. The idea is to fill the bulletin board so thoroughly that you will not have to line it or put a border on it, it will literally be filled with images of active older adults—reading to children, walking, cooking, traveling, and more. Use an open stapler to attach these cutouts to the bulletin board.

If you cannot use a stapler or if you do not have a bulletin board, take a sheet of butcher paper or some other wide paper and cut it to fit the area you want to fill. Then you can glue or tape the pictures to the paper and secure the paper to the board or wall with thumbtacks or tape. Once the area is covered, take bright letters and spell out your announcement on top of the pictures.

Enlist some of the older adults to help you with this project. Invite the helpers to join you for a few hours as you begin to cut and attach the pictures. This will give you and them another opportunity to get to know each other.

You can even enlist the children in your church to help with the publicity. Provide the children with construction paper that has been folded like a standard-sized birthday card. Ask them to color a bright picture about singing in the church or about how much they like to sing on the outside. Design an invitation that can be photocopied and cut to fit the card. Have the children glue the invitation into each card, and then put the cards in envelopes. These can then be mailed to all prospective members, or for even more fun and excitement, help the children "deliver" these cards during Sunday school. If the children have signed the cards, they may even receive a note in return.

When you involve many people in a project, you build interest and a real sense of being part of something new and exciting. Other intergenerational ideas are shared in chapter 6.

Chapter Three
The Older Voice—Subject
to Change

If you were to begin learning how to play a musical instrument, such as the violin, one of the first things you would learn is how to hold the instrument in order to play it correctly. The voice is also a kind of instrument. It most closely resembles a wind instrument.

Some members of your new choir may have sung in various choirs in the church for many years. For others, the choral experience will be a new one. One goal of any choral endeavor is to produce a good choral tone and to sing words that are clearly understood. Phrasing is another important element of choral sound. This chapter is devoted to identifying, correcting, and improving certain elements within the choral sound of your choir.

The human voice is a true gift. Through it we are able to find and use words of affection and encouragement, compassion and expression. We alone are responsible for the way we care for and use this marvelous instrument.

Wobble

Certain physical conditions affect the way the voice produces sound. One word often heard in describing the older adult singing voice is *wobbly*. I wish this were another stereotype, but unfortunately it tends to be closer to fact than to fiction in the untrained choir. No one can completely explain why this wobble occurs; nor can we completely get rid of it. We do know that at some point it is part of the older voice. However, there are some things we can teach our singers to help control this problem.

As directors we can sometimes help straighten the tone by the way we use our gesture as we direct. As you direct, imagine that your flat hand is an iron and sweep it side to side as if you were ironing. Explain to the choir that when they see this gesture they should try to straighten or smooth the sound. If you have a particularly strong wobble present, you can even ask your choir to practice a familiar passage using their hands as "irons." This may not completely correct the problem of the wobble, but it can help.

Breathing

Proper breathing for a singer is a matter of conditioning. The whole body must be conditioned in order to be able to breathe properly. Older adults today know the importance of being physically active. In most shopping malls you can find groups of various ages who meet and walk every day. Normal aging will reduce lung capacity, but capacity may be retained by daily exercising. Walking for even thirty minutes every other day will help improve physical condition and therefore make breathing easier. There are also exercises that can be done in a chair, in a seated position. Nothing will completely counteract the effects of aging on the lungs, but a daily exercise routine definitely will improve each singer's ability to breathe.

Posture directly affects the breathing. Before you begin any simple exercises with your choir, check to see just how they are sitting. Are they slouched in the chairs or sitting with legs crossed?

Ask the singers to plant both feet on the floor, with one

foot slightly in front of the other, in a comfortable position. Then ask them to imagine that they are marionettes. Have them picture a string attached to the top of the head and one attached to the breastbone. Then, tell them to imagine that these strings are being pulled gradually tighter until the head becomes straight and the chest slowly rises. Next, ask them to imagine that the strings are pulling them slightly toward the front. This simple exercise will help to put the body in a better position to breathe properly. Start slowly as you begin to introduce better posture. Your members may not be able to hold this position throughout the rehearsal. Some may not be able to achieve this new position completely, but even a slight improvement will help with breath control.

Think for a moment about the way you are breathing right now. Are you using a majority of your lungs, or do you sense that only a small portion is being used? Now take a deep and cleansing breath. This is done by breathing in deeply through the nose and then expelling the breath gradually through the mouth. Using correct posture and introducing the cleansing breath exercise will help the singer to understand just how to control these muscles.

Part of controlled breathing involves learning to control how fast the breath is expelled. Ask your choir to stand, take a deep breath, and slowly expel this breath. When a person has expelled all of the air, he or she is to sit down. Everyone starts off standing, and as they release all of their air, they will sit one at a time. This exercise can become something of a competition with everyone wanting to be among the last ones standing. This is also another way to teach proper breath control without announcing, "Now let's practice breathing!"

Warm-ups

Warm-ups are especially important to a novice choir. They help to prepare the voice to move from speaking to singing. They also enable the singer to begin to control and improve his or her range of notes.

Begin with simple exercises using syllables and gradually work your way up and down the keyboard.

Exercise No. 1

No _____   No   No   No   No   No   No   No

Exercise No. 2

Ha   Ha   Ha   Ha   Ha   Ha   Ha   Ha   Ha   Ha   Ha   Ha   Ha

After your choir has become accustomed to using these simple exercises, try the following one. It uses a variety of syllables, intervals, and phrasing. You will need to provide your singers with a photocopy of all of the exercises you will use, make posters of them, or write them on a board so that you can refer to them easily.

Range

Begin working with the singer's middle range. In a new choir you do not want to select anthems in which the soprano or tenor would be stretching to reach the top notes or one in which your alto or bass voices would be struggling to control a very low note. You achieve good choral tones by developing the middle, more comfortable, notes.

Start with the exercises discussed earlier. These can be used to stretch and control the singers' range, but initially use them to strengthen the middle register.

Problems with pitch may be directly related to a singer's efforts to support tones that are not within easy reach and to improper breathing. Older adults who have limited breath control can experience a note going gradually flat over a period of measures. If a singer has limited breath control, she or he will have difficulty continuing a phrase for more than four or five measures. Running out of air at the end of the phrase can cause the sound to go slightly flat. Forcing the sound in the upper register often results in going slightly sharp.

The first step in correcting a pitch problem is to have the singers intentionally *listen* to the sounds around them. You may discover that one or more of your choir members is singing too loudly. Without calling attention to one person, suggest to the choir that if they can hear the parts being sung around them, *then* they are singing in a balanced manner. If this listening does not help initially with the choir in a seated position, ask them to stand in a circle facing the middle. As they sing a familiar passage, gesture to soften any section of the circle that is singing too loudly. It is through listening to the others around us that we begin to develop a good choral blend as well as correcting some pitch problems.

Here is an exercise you can use to help train the singers' ears to hear and correct pitch problems. Play a starting pitch and ask the singers to sing the pitch back to you. Next, play a pitch that is a third above the starting pitch. Explain that the choir will sing the first pitch on "ah," then, over a period of four to eight beats, gradually raise the pitch to the interval a third above. This is a difficult exercise to convey to a new choir and one you would not want to introduce at your first rehearsals. But if there is a pitch problem, this exercise can begin to develop the choral ear of your choir.

Phrasing

When it comes to phrasing within a choral group, the director is the one in charge. The choir will need to learn what your gestures are conveying. For this to happen, you must first be as familiar with the musical score as possible. As you study your score, look for possible problem spots and mark them on the page. Pay attention to the line of the music and the texts. Remember, phrases are musical sentences. For the music to be clearly understood (both music and text), you must know where you want to put the "periods" in the line or where it would be better to continue the sound rather than breaking.

A rule that is fundamental to any kind of teaching is simply: "Learn first, then teach!" It is up to you to teach the choir how to present any anthem in good choral form. I cannot overemphasize the importance of knowing the score before you begin to teach.

The gesture of the director is like the brush of a great artist. The gesture actually helps the choir to paint a musical picture in a variety of styles. Even if you direct from a piano or organ, you must be aware of the cues you give to the choir. There are a number of books for directors who want to improve their skills. A new one from Abingdon Press is *Upbeat Downbeat* by Sandra Willetts. This book is written in concise and clear terminology and can be a good resource for a new director.

Chapter Four
Selecting Music to Inspire and Encourage

From your initial meetings with older adults, when you offered to lead some singing, you had an idea of what kind of hymns they like to sing. This knowledge will help you plan the first rehearsal.

Hymn Arrangements

Some of these favorite hymns should be part of your first choir experience. The hymns will be music that your choir has sung for many years, music with which they feel most comfortable and confident. *The United Methodist Hymnal* contains a wealth of hymns that may be used as simple anthems, introits, prayer responses, or solos.

There are a number of ways you can arrange a hymn as an anthem or a special piece of service music (introit, prayer response, and so on.) straight out of the hymnal. In *The United Methodist Hymnal* on selection 57, the hymn *O For a Thousand Tongues to Sing,* is one of the best known and most loved hymns of United Methodists and is often viewed as Methodism's own song.

Your new choir will have sung this piece often during their years within the church. They may even know most of the words by memory. Ask the altos, tenors, and basses to sing the unison melody line with very full and supported voices. After they have sung the first verse to your satisfaction, turn to your sopranos and announce that they will be singing the alto line of music, one octave higher than is written. Demonstrate what you have asked for them to do, as you play the alto line one octave higher. Next ask the sopranos to sing with you, again as you play the alto line.

The alto line is not difficult to learn, even members who do not read music will feel confident within a very short time. When the sopranos are comfortable with this new descant, ask the other choir members to sing the melody with the sopranos' new line. In a matter of minutes your choir will have learned an old hymn in a new way and will have gained a wonderful, yet simple choral call to worship or introit. An older adult who does not read music may feel timid about singing even a simple anthem, but will feel confident when working on a familiar hymn.

When the singer does not know how to read music, you will need to teach any piece of music by rote. This is why demonstrating the soprano line described above was so important. The line was short, very rhythmic and defined. Even the non-music reading singer would be able to imitate you after a very short time. Teaching by rote takes more time and patience. But if you find that this is the only way you can begin, try to include some basic music training, such as recognizing certain intervals or note values.

There are a number of hymns and responses in the hymnal that can be used for a variety of service music, but now let us look at how you can take a simple spiritual and turn it into an anthem. Number 704 in the hymnal, *Steal Away to Jesus,* is already arranged in good choral form. By making just a few changes to some notes (timing), adding phrase marks and dynamic markings, as well as indicating three short solos, you will have a good anthem.

If you do not have a hymnal that is your own, try to get one. Put your name on the inside and the outside (I use white correcting fluid to write my last name on the outside). When

Steal Away to Jesus

WORDS: African American spiritual
MUSIC: African American spiritual; adapt. and arr. by William Farley Smith
Adapt. and arr. © 1989 The United Methodist Publishing House

STEAL AWAY
57.58 with Refrain

you have a hymnal that will be only yours, you are then free to mark changes and make notes on each page. The example on page 37 comes directly from my personal hymnal.

Notice that I did not change the pitches of the notes. I made a few changes to note durations, and I added some well-placed dynamic markings. I also included three short solos, using only the first phrase of each stanza as the other choir members sang their part on "ooh" or "ah." These changes can be explained to your choir, so that they can mark them (in pencil) in the choir hymnals, or they are simple enough for you simply to convey as you direct. If you want to make a copy out of your book for the choir, you will need to contact the publisher to obtain permission.

There are a number of song collections that your choir will enjoy using. Any Christian bookstore will have several from which to choose. A few years ago I found a book titled *Awaken Your Heart: New Songs for the Spiritual Journey and New Texts with Familiar Hymn Tunes* in my local Cokesbury bookstore. I immediately noticed that there were a number of texts that would speak to, and of, the lives of older adults. There were a number of new texts set to familiar tunes.

I have found that when working with a new choir, if I can find a song that uses a familiar tune, I can gain the confidence and participation of the group quickly. The hymns "Create Us New" and "Come People, Gather and Rejoice" (found in the Resource section of this book) are examples of traditional hymn tunes being put together with new texts.

When selecting music for older adults, I look for texts that reflect experiences in their lives. During our lifetime, numerous changes occur that evoke a variety of emotions. The older we become, the more change we have experienced. Older adults have reached that age when one of these changes is loss: loss of friends; loss of certain freedoms; and perhaps loss of lifestyle. I find that I am constantly searching for those texts that not only affirm older adults but also affirm their ability to cope with change. Often encouragement may be found in remembering and celebrating the past. There are a number of hymns in *The United Methodist Hymnal* that celebrate those who have been part of our church family and have now died. Others celebrate the acts of daily life shared by all Christians. In the Resource section of this book is a partial listing of these hymns as well as the text of an appropriate new hymn, "Through All the Years."

In 1975 the Hymn Society of America, at the request of the Church Relations Department of the National Retired Teachers Association and the American Association of Retired Persons, launched a search for hymns that would celebrate the later years of a person's life and that would address the meaning of age. More than 1200 texts were submitted. A booklet was compiled with ten of these new hymns. Examples from this booklet may be found in the Resource section as well as information needed to order the booklet.

Purchased Octavos

Once you know the musical ability of your new choir, you may decide to purchase a few octavos. In the Resource section you will find several music houses that specialize in mail order and provide customers with excellent catalogs of available music.

As you look through one of these catalogs you will discover that music is available for every kind of voicing—(unison, two-part, SAB, SATB, and so on). Once you determine the edition needed, you can select a variety of music that will work for your choir. In recent years, a number of excellent simplified editions of certain classics have become available. These may be perfect for the newly formed choir. Hal Hopson is one composer who has mastered the art of taking classic pieces and simplifying them in such a way that they do not lose the quality of the original. His arrangements include the music of J. S. Bach and Mozart and are arranged in either two-part or SAB form. These arrangements may be found in a good music catalog that lists pieces by composer/arranger.

Another writer to explore is Fred Bock. Mr. Bock arranged Schubert's "Holy, Holy, Holy" for an SAB choir. The arrangement is simple, clear, and the character of the piece is still present. It is a piece that will require more work and time to learn than something from the hymnal or something familiar, but it is sure to become a worthwhile part of your choir repertoire.

Your choir should begin to build a basic repertoire of familiar and new pieces with varying degrees of difficulty. These songs should reflect different styles and themes. The choir's favorites should be included.

Several of the examples cited here have been written not only *for* older adults but *by* older adults. Some of your choir members may write lyrics or poetry. If you discover a hidden talent, celebrate it! These are gifts to be used.

Chapter Five
Organization of the Older Adult Choir

Delegate Those Jobs!

Once your choir has been formed, never lose sight of the fact that a good choir experience occurs *with* the members and not *for* the members. If you are constantly trying to do everything for everyone, your choir will not have the level of ownership that they need and you will be exhausted trying to find enough hours in the day to take care of all kinds of details.

Electing choir officers or assigning specific duties to members need not take place as soon as the choir is formed. After the first or second rehearsal, begin by assigning small ad hoc committees to be responsible for various areas, such as, attendance and follow-up, transportation, refreshments, and recruitment, to name a few.

After the choir has met for a while, you will begin to see some persons assuming leadership roles. This is the moment to suggest electing officers and assigning specific people to be responsible for the various committees. Your choir will be able to determine the kinds of officers and committees that will foster a functional and nurturing group.

Let the entire choir participate in selecting a nominating committee whose job will be to propose a slate of officers. This committee should make sure that the persons nominated are willing to accept the responsibility. When elections are held make sure that the choir members are aware that they can nominate people from the floor for these positions or adopt the proposed slate from the nominations committee. Establish how long these positions will be held. In an older adult group, short terms are often easier for persons to handle. Six-month or even quarterly terms may work best for your group.

Officers

Every group needs a **president,** who will preside at brief business meetings and help coordinate the various committees. Also necessary are a **secretary** to help keep the choir records, a **treasurer** to handle the collected funds of the choir, a **publicity chairman,** a **librarian,** and possibly a **host** and **hostess,** or **entertainment chairperson.**

Several of these officers would be in charge of committees. For example, the **librarian** could have a committee of persons who would meet regularly to file, repair, catalog, or distribute the music you have selected for use. This committee would also be responsible for having a new-member folder of music ready for guests who drop into the rehearsals.

The **host/hostess** or **entertainment chairperson** would be responsible for greeting the members and guests as they enter the choir room, securing refreshments for after the rehearsal, recruiting volunteers to help set up coffee or other beverages, and clean up after refreshments have been served. This person(s) would also plan seasonal gatherings or parties and even secure outside entertainment for the group.

The **secretary** may have a small committee to help send out birthday cards and postcards to members who have missed a rehearsal and to assist with telephone responsibilities. A telephone committee provides a wonderful opportunity for people in the choir who cannot help in other ways to reach out to fellow members.

The **treasurer** is responsible for administering the funds collected from the choir. This money can go toward a flower or "sunshine" fund or support various choir mission projects. A choir may decide to "pass the plate" to receive additional funds; or, the group may establish dues for members. Let the members decide which is best; they know firsthand what their individual budgets can handle.

If a **transportation chairperson** is elected, he or she makes sure that everyone who needs a ride to choir rehearsal or events receives it. This person might arrange carpools or coordinate with the church office to meet the needs of the older adults.

The **publicity chairperson** is responsible for making sure all choir members know of activities and extra rehearsals. This person also is responsible for publicizing choir events to the church and community.

A **choir historian** is a great addition to a new choir. This person can begin to document in pictures and clippings from newsletters or newspapers the story of the group and the individuals within it. The historian should be good with a camera or have a partner who enjoys taking pictures. A choir scrapbook can hold all of this important information.

An **activity chairperson** works with a committee to plan social events of all kinds for the group. Older adults don't just want to rehearse and participate in worship. They want to go! They want to go into the community and be involved in service projects; they want to go and serve as friendly visitors to homebound people or nursing home residents; they want to do things with each other. The choir can become a real community or family. This group could plan day trips, holiday activities, nights out, and more.

When jobs are delegated, some very positive results begin to take place. First, the older adult is not just an honored guest but a hands-on participant. He or she begins to see that part of the success of this group is his or her responsibility. As people work together, a bond of caring is created. The older adult has had to deal with a number of life changes. This kind of bond can provide a substitute for the family, if their own family lives far away; it can provide new friends, as old friends move away or die. The older adult gains a sense of community in which there is room for self-expression and creativity.

The list of committees and officers could go on indefinitely. Assess the needs of your own situation and with help from your choir decide what jobs need to be filled.

As you establish responsibilities within the group, do remember to include **devotional leaders.** These persons help to plan brief devotions or to secure other devotional leaders. There are many faith stories within the older adult choir. Give your members the opportunity to share these stories with their choir family.

A prayer chain is essential to nurturing this community. The prayer chain should be a volunteer-only group; no one should be forced to be part of it. After the sign-up period is completed, divide the group into several sections with no more than five or six members in each. When a prayer request becomes known, either you or some other designated person calls the first person in each section; then that person calls the next, and so on, until all members are contacted.

Once you have given the choir an opportunity to be responsible for certain tasks, you can be free to reach out to any members who have trouble finding their way into the fellowship. You may notice someone who is rather shy or withdrawn; perhaps he or she cannot hear very well or for some other reason seems to be on the outside edges of the group. Do not be surprised, though, to learn that a choir member who is less involved really likes it that way. There are some older adults who prefer to be observers, and that is fine. They may be at a stage when they choose not to be in the middle of an activity. If possible, find a number of very limited projects for these persons to work on, such as decorations, making banners, or gathering toiletries or special treats for those members who may be homebound for a limited time.

An outgrowth of an older adult choir may be a committee that influences the life of the church in a broader way. Considering the increase in the older adult population and the capacity of most older adults to be involved and active not only in their own lives but also in the life of their church, your choir may decide to follow the example of the 1992 General Conference of The United Methodist Church and establish a Council on Older Adult Ministries.

In 1992 the General Conference approved the formation of a Committee on Older Adult Ministries. This committee is made up of one member from each of the various boards and agencies in the church, one bishop, and one representative from each jurisdiction. A local church council would be composed of a member from all the various committees and work areas, the senior pastor, and one older adult from each of the stages discussed in chapter 1 (young-old, middle-old, and old-old).

The purpose of such a council is to share information, coordinate joint programs, serve as an advocate for older adult issues and ministries, and promote a growing, inclusive ministry for all persons.

This council could help shape the way your church views the older adult in the future. It could provide opportunities for enrichment of and leadership by the older adults in the local church. It could be a vehicle of communication among all ages for an intentional ministry.

Think for a long time about this kind of council. This is not an idea to be taken lightly. A Council on Older Adult Ministries can change the way we view all the members of the local church. When you have thought this through, take the idea to someone else, perhaps the pastor or another leader. Together, begin a dialogue about the possibility of forming a Committee on Older Adult Ministries. Every good program begins with one idea that then becomes a possibility in the hands of church. If you have a successful older adult choir organization, this may be the time for the idea to become the possibility that will become the focus for the future.

Chapter Six
All Together—An
Intergenerational Approach

One evening a choir member came into my office before our rehearsal. She told me about a trip that our church's older adult group (Spice of Life) had taken and about some of the places they had seen. She explained that at one rest stop there was quite a long line waiting to go into the restroom. As the ladies were waiting, a door opened and a young mother with a daughter about six or seven years of age came out. The daughter looked at the group of older adults and turning to her mother had asked, "Why are their faces so old?"

My friend and I shared a chuckle together over the things children say that embarrass their parents. But as I thought about that story, I realized that this child apparently had not been around very many older adults. Perhaps she was not able to be with her grandparents. How sad!

I thought of my own grandmother and the wonderful experiences we shared. And then I remembered a story my mother would tell when "Mimi" retired the first time. Mimi had been a bookkeeper and was proud that she rarely used an adding machine when she was working on her books.

Mimi decided to retire and spend more time with her two granddaughters. What had sounded good at first became an emotional roller coaster for our family.

Mimi would dress as if she were going to work and arrive at our house everyday before breakfast. She would spend every minute with my mother, her daughter. This situation soon became a nightmare for us all. Fortunately, my Mother realized that it was as much a problem for Mimi as it was for us. This story illustrates a transition that can really shake a family more than the departure of a grown child—a retirement within the family.

As we move through our middle-age years and into the younger older adult age, our lives have a certain continuity about them, a certain order or sameness. It is a comfortable feeling. Retirement may seem like a golden age as you look forward to it, but it can suddenly tarnish if that certain order and continuity are changed or gone.

Mimi was retired the first time for two weeks when she decided to see if she could work at her church just a little every week. It was not long until Mimi was a bookkeeper again, proudly showing people that she did not need an adding machine and would never use a calculator.

When Mimi began working at the church, she also began to meet and know some of the children in the preschool program. She delighted in telling the family how these children would make a "special visit" to see her and bring little gifts, like cookies or pictures. My sister and I did the same kinds of things, but this relationship with the children in her church was different.

What none of us realized at the time was that these "special visits" probably had been planned by a sensitive leader who knew the value of nurturing intergenerational communication and experiences. Interaction with others is one of the best ways for us to expand our own experience. Intergenerational contacts give us a glimpse of what the future may hold and can help us to be more effective as we approach it. If communication and experience can be cultivated between the older person and the younger, each will find reason to be encouraged, challenged, and reassured.

Working with Children

Consider a cooperative project to bring together the older adult choir and children's choir in your church. If you are the minister or director of music for the church, you may even be the leader of both groups! Should someone else be the leader of the children's group, consider approaching this person with the idea of cultivating some shared experiences.

A joint work would be an excellent first-time venture, and it will be an adventure! It should have a definite beginning and a definite time to end. You may choose to work on a musical or cantata (refer to bibliography), or you may decide that a concert would be more appropriate. Once you have agreed on the best endeavor, the work and fun can begin.

Begin with separate rehearsals. While the older adults may enjoy some of the antics of a children's choir rehearsal, they probably would not enjoy it over a long period of time. Also, you should be speaking differently to children than you do to older adults.

One of the objects of a joint endeavor is to create ways for the two groups to get to know one another and develop a dialogue. If they are practicing separately, you will need to find a way to begin building communication for the day when the groups come together.

Everyone enjoys getting a surprise in the mail, whether a letter, a card, or even a gift or treat. Children and older adults are no different. Children will race to see if something has come for them in the mail. I have known many older adults who feel the same way and are disappointed when the box is empty.

One way to help the children and older adults begin to know one another is to establish pen pals. Check with both groups to see if there is anyone who does not want to participate and then assign the pals. If there are not enough participants for everyone to have one pen pal, then assign two writers to one. Be sure that the older adults who want to participate are literate. If someone is unable to read or write, then work to find a partner for him or her. The pen pals can exchange small crafts they have made or pictures they have drawn. They could even start coloring a picture together by mail. To do this activity, you or the pal would send a picture to be colored to the other pal. Together they would take turns coloring and mailing the picture back and forth. Small gifts such as bookmarks or perfume samples may be exchanged. The possibilities are endless.

You may be wondering just how expensive all of this mailing is going to be. If you let the choir rehearsal of each group be the place where the items are "mailed," then you or one of your helpers can be the "mail carrier" at the next rehearsal and deliver the mail. If you choose to do this project, you will need to make sure that no one stops participating without your knowledge.

Another project is joint photo display. Make pictures of all the members of both choirs. Post these on an attractive bulletin board or poster. Under each picture clearly print the person's name and perhaps the month of his or her birth or something that person likes to do.

Both of these projects are geared to make that first joint rehearsal a time of discovery personally as well as musically. Any project should help the members of your group have an easier time getting to know one another. At the first joint rehearsal, especially if the children will be meeting the older adults for the first time, plan for a refreshment time prior to the practice. Make name tags for everyone. If you have pictures of the individuals put them face down on a table or in a bag (one for the older adults and one for the children) and then ask the children to draw out one picture and find that person. This will create a rush of activity as the youngsters try to find "their person." The information on the picture will help start conversation. When this first flurry has died down, ask the children to sit down and let the older adults go through the same process. Every person should have made at least two new friends and you have not had to announce, "Now let's mingle!"

Once the two choirs are seated, practice several of your songs. Also, let each group sing for the other. These activities will foster that caring bond between the two groups discussed in earlier chapters. The children and the older adults will begin to listen and learn from each other. A bond may also form between the parents of these children and the older adults they might not have known.

Many benefits can come from activities such as the ones above. The children and the older adults benefit from being with each other. They become more aware of the needs of every age. Each group will have the opportunity to develop a positive image of the other's capabilities. Stereotypes begin to vanish as the older adults are seen in new and different ways. It's possible that a children who is not able to be with his or her grandparents and a grandparent without a grandchild close by may establish a special bond.

Working with Youth

You may determine that a joint effort between the teenagers in your church and the older adults would be a better venture. Some of the same projects already described can be adapted, but when you are involving teens some very unique projects can be undertaken. The youth and older adults might mix a mission-oriented project with the music one. On joint work days both groups could come together to tackle projects within the church building, such as painting or sorting in the library or kitchen. They might even decide to work on home projects of some homebound church members.

These kinds of "working together" projects produce benefits similar to those mentioned, but there is something even more special in the relationship between teens and older adults. Each group is dealing with certain questions of self-esteem. Teens and older adults face some of the same fears, such as fear of failure or fear of not being accepted. The teenager struggles to find his or her own place in family, church, school, and society. The older adult seeks a redefined place in family, church, and society. Sharing their perspectives on these life changes can be an enriching experience for both groups. Every stage, every age of life has gifts we all need to discover and cherish.

Chapter Seven
Time to Share—Time to Serve

Older adults who are looking for ways to be of service in their local church want to do more than just fill their time. The older adults I have known want to be involved in an intentional and purposeful ministry. Ministry that is focused and intentional will enable the older adult to continue growing, spiritually and mentally, throughout old age.

A choir can be that intentional ministry sought by the older adult. It provides an excellent opportunity to serve the local church on a regular basis within the worship service. The choir can be scheduled for a variety of services throughout the year. They may present a musical or sacred concert or be in a joint musical venture as discussed in chapter 6.

An Older Adult Worship Service

Your church may never have devoted an entire Sunday service toward celebrating the lives of the older adults in the congregation. A thematic service like this is easily planned and can open the eyes of the total congregation to the abilities and gifts of the older members. The month of May is National Senior Citizens Month, a good month to plan such a special service.

Before you begin to involve others in planning a worship service, first meet with your pastor. Discuss with him or her the goal of such a service. Then with pastoral approval and participation, you can begin to make definite plans. Let your choir help to plan this older adult Sunday. An entire older adult service (especially one during a formal worship hour) should not be planned until you have met as a choir for several months. Knowing and working together during these first months will help everyone begin to recognize certain gifts and graces within the group.

As you begin to plan the service, consider the various elements that denote a particular service. For a morning worship service, for instance, you would need a copy of the order of service to guide the planning.

For a celebration of the older adults, make sure the congregation is aware that "something different" is really happening. Perhaps the choir could process during the prelude or singing of the first hymn. Banners could be made in advance and displayed. These banners would celebrate the work of the older adults in the local church or the lives of older adults in the Bible, such as Sarah and Moses. Special bulletin covers featuring older adults in ministry could be made or purchased.

These elements are like scenery in the theater: they help the play—or worship service—take shape and become focused but they are not the most important part of the experience. You don't want to walk out of a theater saying, "Wasn't the scenery pretty." You want to leave knowing that you have experienced the play, that it has touched you. The same is true of the older adult worship service. This service should not be simply a visual presentation. The people in the pews should leave knowing their lives have been touched in a special—and sometimes profound—way.

Your pastor may encourage and help you find an older adult to deliver the sermon. If you cannot find an individual to take this responsibility, try to find several who are willing to share their faith stories. Your choir is filled with amazing stories of faith that can be uplifting to all who hear them.

The music for this service will act to continue the theme and will bring together all of the elements within the service. This would be an excellent time to use hymns that have been written by older adults (see Resources). Enlist persons willing to serve as liturgists or readers, collect tithes, lead the congregation in corporate prayers, and to make the announcements for the day. The Resources section suggests a variety of worship aids.

Within the district and annual conference there are many ways the older adult may serve. In my own conference (Holston) we hold an Older Adult Rally each spring. On a given day, across the conference at various locations older adults gather for workshops, classes, worship, informal singing, lunch, and entertainment.

Retreats for older adults are offered in most areas. If the older adults you work with are able to make a longer trip, check some specialized retreat centers, such as Lake Junaluska in North Carolina, to learn about older adult weekends held throughout the year. Scarritt-Bennett Center in Nashville, Tennessee is another place that offers planned and guided workshops and retreats for the older adult.

Your choir would also enjoy participating in activities sponsored by the Fellowship of United Methodists in Music, Worship and Other Arts, such as music weeks held during the summer. As your choir becomes more accustomed to singing, consider contacting the worship committee of your annual conference to see if the older adult choir could sing during one of the worship services.

Planning a Choir Trip

Once your choir has built up its repertoire, investigate possibilities for a choir tour at the end of the choir year. This kind of trip will give the older adult choir the opportunity to share their own special story and spread the joy of being an older Christian.

Before any commitments are made for the choir, be sure

they are interested in working toward a choir tour. I would be very surprised if they did not want to plan this kind of endeavor. Remember, the older adult is actively looking for the opportunity to serve and to minister to others. Choir members usually see a tour as an excellent opportunity.

A successful choir tour involves more than a good program. It requires intense planning of every element or aspect of the trip. The remainder of this chapter will describe what to consider as you arrange a choir tour.

You may know of several locations where your choir could sing, such as retirement centers, daycare facilities, elementary schools, festivals, malls, or other churches, to name but a few. As you consider how far you want to travel and how long you will be gone, you may decide that you will not need outside help in planning the trip. However, if you would rather take the easier way, a travel agent can plan the details of the trip itself. The American Association of Retired Persons (AARP) can also help you plan a great trip. A professional will have experience in planning trips for many ages. He or she will know of side trips the choir could make on the way to a singing engagement or of unique places to stop for meals or shopping. There may be a nominal fee to use a travel agent, but most often agents are paid a commission from the hotels and transportation companies with whom they negotiate their trips. If a travel professional is not going to be used, you can still plan a wonderful trip by using your contacts in the various areas where your choir will be singing.

One of the first decisions to be made is how the group will travel. If your church has a vehicle large enough to accommodate your group, this would be the most economical method. If a church vehicle is not available, decide whether driving private cars is feasible or if you prefer to rent a bus. The bus would be the most expensive way to go, but it would be the most comfortable for the older adults. They would have access to a bathroom and would be able to enjoy the sights and each other.

If you decide to use cars belonging to choir members, think through the trip and plan carefully. Do not let your group travel in a "caravan." Trying to travel together can create dangerous driving situations and can contribute to delays. Rather, provide the travelers with a map of the route to be taken, the hour they will need to arrive, the location of the place where the group will gather, and the amount of time it will take to get there. Also include the phone number of the destination in case someone should have car trouble or become lost. If your trip will cover several days, give the drivers new directions every day, or make sure to mark clearly on the itinerary where the tour will go on each day.

Secure copies of all auto insurance papers, driver's licenses, and car tags on a master sheet. This sheet should also indicate who will be traveling in each car.

Purchase a plastic portable file box with a handle to keep important papers together. From each choir member gather the following information for this file: copies of health insurance cards or numbers, prescriptions, any known medical conditions, the name of their personal physicians, and who to contact in the event of an emergency.

Prepare a small kit for emergencies, including various bandaids and bandages; antibiotic creams and cleansers (alcohol, peroxide); aspirin and nonaspirin pain relievers; antidiarrhea over-the-counter medications; upset stomach medications; instant cold packs, a bloodpressure cuff and stethoscope, comfort items such as lotion, burn cream, and so on. Try to anticipate any need your choir may have.

What to Do When You Arrive

Notify each place where your choir will be singing, that you will arrive one hour prior to the concert. This will give you time to practice in the room where you will be singing and give your choir a chance to stretch after sitting in a car or bus.

The choir should not be expected to stand through each performance. In fact, some of the members may not be able to stand and sing at all. These members may sit in chairs at the front of the choir. Older adult choirs should sing no more than two songs before sitting down. Consider singing several songs from a seated position. Your choir should also not be required to stand on narrow risers during a performance. If a choir loft is not going to be available, then arrange chairs on the floor for your singers.

After the choir has been seated, sing one of their favorite selections. Listen to the way the sound moves within the room. You may need to make adjustments before the program begins. When you are satisfied with the choir arrangement, sing a little of each piece that will be presented during the program.

Try not to work the choir too hard or long before the concert. Give them time to relax or walk around before they have to perform. Prior to going into the performance, gather your group and lead them in a brief devotion and prayer.

Other Things to Consider

How would you handle the death of a choir member on tour? If you are not sure how you would handle this kind of situation or even what needs to be done, speak to a funeral director prior to leaving to know what steps would need to be taken in the event the worst should happen. If a death does occur, minister to your choir. They will look to you for guidance and consolation, and they will then follow your example in dealing with the grief of the group.

Look for ways to make the trip more enjoyable for the choir. If you have time, prepare a Choir Tour Journal for each member before you leave. Each page would contain information about the trip for that day. You could list how many miles will be traveled, the destination, interesting things to be seen through the day. Leave room for the members to make their own notes on each page. This will be a wonderful souvenir of their tour.

If you are traveling by bus, ask your choir to rotate seats at each stop. The older adults would also enjoy a sing-along going down the road. You could use the loudspeaker on the bus to interview the members and have a few games for the group to play. The group will also appreciate some unstructured time to read, rest, or sleep.

Planning a trip for older adults can be time-consuming, but it can also be great fun.

The Older Adult Musical

A musical can be a wonderful opportunity for older adults to share with the congregation the many talents learned during their lifetime. A musical can be incorporated in a choir tour if it can be performed in a variety of various locations with little scenery or set-up.

A number of older adult musicals have been written. In selecting one, consider how many speaking and singing parts there are. Looking at the staging requirements to determine at what points the actors would be able to sit and perform. If everyone in the choir really wants a speaking part, then by all means try to make one available for each. Certain parts could be divided and shared among several individuals, or you can write extra lines.

There is more to a play than just the actors, of course. Many different talents can be employed. Enlist people to build simple scenery and gather items to be used in the staging. Put someone in charge of props. A wardrobe master or mistress can coordinate costuming, whether purchasing, renting, or making costumes. Several of your singers may enjoy a variety of needlecrafts, and you can begin building your own costume wardrobe by using these talents. Assign someone to be in charge of publicity and printing, which includes designing a program cover and perhaps having tickets printed.

As you can see, there are ample jobs for everyone who wants to have one. A musical can be an opportunity to learn and use many talents within the group. It can also be a way for the congregation to experience and appreciate the many abilities of older adults.

Chapter Eight
More Than One Way to
Share a Song

Handbells

An older adult handbell choir is another avenue for the older adult to minister within his or her church. A number of excellent books—available in every Christian bookstore that has a music section—explain how to start a bell choir for children or adults. There are, however, some aspects of beginning an older adult handbell choir that differ from working with any other age group.

Some special equipment may be needed for the older adult in a handbell choir. The older adult may not be able to stand throughout an entire rehearsal. Stools or raised chairs should be provided to enable members to practice from a seated position. These seats should raise the ringer enough so that the bells will not come in contact with the bell table during rehearsal but not so high that reading the music becomes difficult.

In an earlier chapter I discussed the value of large-print music. Handbell music is normally printed in larger notation, but if not, follow some of the same suggestions previously mentioned. Lighting is again a consideration for the practice area. If you have overhead lighting, make sure that none of your ringers have a shadow from their bodies falling across the page. You may need to adjust the room arrangement in order for everyone to have an unobstructed view of the director.

Consider other possible physical limitations of the group. There may be a number of ringers with arthritis in their wrists or fingers. One of my most faithful ringers moved from playing some of the middle bells to playing only the higher, smaller bells due to problems with her wrists. I was pleased that my friend wanted to continue to perform in the bell choir and was always glad to work with her to help find a more comfortable way to perform.

For persons wearing bifocals or trifocals consider purchasing clear plastic raised music stands that hold the music folder about eight inches above the bell table. They are also lightweight and stackable so that you can easily remove them when other groups need to practice.

If the older adults are not able to read music or have very limited musical training, begin by using very simple music involving not more than two octaves. Unison arrangements of familiar hymns are excellent, because the new ringers will be able to hear a familiar line of music and more easily work with the timing. As you teach this novice group, start giving them basic music education: note values; timing (signatures); recognition of note names on the staff, and so forth.

Once the bells have been assigned at the first rehearsal, teach the correct way to ring the bells. From this point begin to introduce note values and rhythm. Work on simple rhythmic exercises with the group. At the first rehearsal you may not even introduce a melody. Make sure the rehearsal has been planned in such a way that by the end the group has successfully played an exercise together. Each rehearsal needs to end with the feeling of accomplishment. This is especially important in a novice older adult group as it will encourage them to come back and continue learning this new art.

Tone Chimes

If your church does not have handbells and you sense a real interest in this kind of choir, tone chimes or hand chimes could be purchased. These instruments are played very much like handbells and use the same music, but chimes are not as fragile as bells. Many churches have both handbells and tone chimes available. The tone chimes are often used to train children how to ring before the bells are introduced. The tones are slightly softer but the technique used in ringing is the same.

A number of octavos have been introduced that include limited bell accompaniment. Consult a good music choral catalog for a list of these titles. Hal Hopson has created a number of these pieces that use as few as four bells. Another choral arrangement that uses just two octaves is "Lord, I Want to Be a Christian," by Mark Cabaniss. In the hymnal are a number of tunes that may be enhanced with simple handbell additions. Natalie Sleeth's piece "Go Now in Peace," number 665, may be played using only bells G 6, C 6, D 6, and G 5. Play this pattern throughout the piece and end with a cluster ring on the last measure. This is not the pattern suggested in the hymnal, but it is a pattern that novice ringers could learn quickly.

Handbells are not the only instruments that an older adult group could utilize. Look at the Sleeth piece again. It is also scored for Orff instruments. These are wooden or metal pitched, percussion instruments. Basic music education needs to be taught as the group learns to play these instruments. There are many books that give information concerning the use of these wonderful instruments. There are also a number of octavos and books available with music written specifically for use with the Orff instruments.

Other Instruments

Many of the older adults you will be working with studied a variety of instruments when they were children and young adults. Some may have played professionally and still enjoy playing but not as often. Older adults are also at a point where they begin to return to private study—either the instruments played when they were younger or an instrument they have always wanted to play.

As you begin to learn what instrumentalists are available in your group, look for ways to include these talents in the choir situation or the worship experience of the church. You may discover a pianist who could accompany the choir. You may even discover enough musicians to build a small instrumental ensemble. This group could learn simple hymn arrangements to share during the worship service. Start simply with the goal of a sense of accomplishment for each musician at the rehearsal.

Older adults enjoy sharing their many talents. It helps both the older adult and the church to realize and affirm the many gifts in the church family. I hope this book has given you the seed to begin a ministry of older adults in your church. This ministry has blessed my life for many years. I find a special beauty and spirit within the older adult community. Working with older adults will teach you a lot about yourself and what you can expect to experience as you also enter the older adult years. My own perceptions on aging have changed, not through reading but through observation. These perceptions continue to change.

Working with older adults is a never-ending adventure! I hope you enjoy your adventure as much as I have mine.

Resources

A Parable Paraphrased

Matthew 25:35

And Jesus said through a parable to the older adult:

"I was hungry and you gave me food."
We were the family down the street who had been without
work for many months. We were hungry and you provided us
with food. You freely gave whenever you saw a need and
expected nothing in return.

"I was thirsty and you gave me drink."
I was the baby boomer who was unchurched and thirsty for
something I could not find. You showed me how to quench my
thirst within the fellowship of your church.

"I was a stranger and you welcomed me."
I was the single parent living alone in a strange, new city.
You became a surrogate grandparent to my child and showed
me how to be a better parent by your example.

"I was naked and you clothed me."
I was the elementary child who could not read. Every day
my classmates could see my lack of skills. You came and
worked with me every day after school. You wrapped me in
the cloak of knowledge.

"I was sick and you visited me."

I was a stroke victim trapped in a body that would not function, even though my mind was still whole. You came and shared in loving witness that recovery was possible. You showed me how to adapt in watching how you have had to adapt.

"I was in prison and you visited me."

I was locked in the prison of depression. You came and showed me the way to recovery by giving myself in meaningful service to others.

And then the older adult shall say, "Lord, when did I see you without work and help you? And when did I see you as a single parent in a strange city? Or the school child needing skills to keep up with the class? And when did I see you trapped in a body that no longer functioned? Or in the prison of depression and showed you the way to freedom in living?"

And the Lord shall say: "Truly, I say to you, as you did it unto the least of these my brothers and sisters, you did it unto me."

Written by Betsy Styles, 1991. Used by permission.

Sending Forth

The word *gerontology* is based on the root word *geros* from the Greek language. The pronunciation of this word is important!

If pronounced "GEros" it means "old."

If pronounced "gerOS" it means "strong."

It all depends on the emphasis put on different syllables!

As you go out in the church and the world to serve, *remember* the difference between "old" and "strong" is only a matter of emphasis—your emphasis!

By Randy Boldt, Waco, Texas. As printed in Agenda. *Used by permission.*

A Responsive Reading

(Inspired by the idea of Rev. Jason Nyaga, Africa, and written by Betsy Styles)

You shall rise in the presence of grey hairs, give honor to the aged and fear your God. (Lev. 19:32)

LORD, HAVE MERCY UPON US.

I have been young and now I am old and never have I seen a righteous man forsaken. (Ps. 37:25)

LORD, TEACH ME TO TRUST YOU.

Do not cast me off when old age comes nor forsake me when my strength fails. (Ps. 71:9)

LORD, IN YOU I PUT MY TRUST.

The glory of young men is their strength, the dignity of old men is their grey hair. (Prov. 20:29)

LORD, LET ME SPEND MY LIFE IN YOUR GLORY.

How can I be sure of this: I am an old man and my wife is well on in years. (Luke 1:18)

REVEAL YOUR GLORY TO ME, O, LORD.

TEACH US TO ORDER OUR DAYS RIGHTLY THAT
WE MAY ENTER THE GATES OF WISDOM.

Litanies

A Litany of Thanksgiving

L: For the gifts of each age and generation,

P: We give you thanks, O Lord.

L: For all those saints who have endowed us with their
faith, their hope, and their wisdom that future generations
might build on their firm foundations,

P: We give you thanks, O Lord.

L: For all your living sages, bestowing gifts of time, energy and persistence beyond the lure of recognition or personal
gain,

P: We give you thanks, O Lord.

L: For Abraham and Sarah, for Elizabeth and Zechariah,
who refused to believe that the generative power of God lay
confined to some preconceived age in life or generation of discipleship,

P: We give you thanks, O Lord.

L: For Simeon and Anna, who were not afraid to exude
their joy in recognition of God's revealing act of salvation
within the human family,

P: We give you thanks, O Lord.

L: For Mary and Joseph, parents who came to knowledge
that God's love and creative energy might engender salvation
beyond even the accepted norms of traditional family values,

P: We give you thanks, O Lord.

L: To lifelong faithful companions and to human examples
of those, who through dependence upon your grace, have
gained the courage to rebuild broken lives and rekindle the mis-
directed flame of love to bind hearts anew and regenerate hope,

P: Give afresh your healing power.

L: For all your beloved who no longer find it within their power to run and not be weary, to walk and not faint, and to all those for whom the lack of speech or hearing or sight or mobility has always presented a barrier to full participation in work and worship, those who nonetheless continue to seek your face and sing your praises in their hearts,

P: Give afresh your healing power.

L: In the inquisitiveness of children, the simple gifts of costumed cherubs and bathrobed shepherds, courageously reminding their elders of the wonder surrounding the miracle of a child's birth as well as the childlike creativity which Christ called forth from all his disciples,

P: You have renewed in us hope, O God.

L: Through all the teaching and learning that take place in life sharing and hand-to-hand skill sharing, in classrooms of brick and mortar, around campfires or beneath branches of pine and oak, in yearly pageants and oratories, in our human built sanctuaries reverberating with bells and pipes and voices raised each week in adoration,

P: You restore our faith by timeless love.

Creator, Redeemer, and Sustainer of us all, help us to embrace the precious offerings of each of your kingdom children. Let us pass peace, hope, and love to each new generation, that every stranger who may wander lost or shaken into the midst of your people may sense the comfort and acceptance of your Son, our Savior, Jesus Christ. Amen.

A Litany of Confession

L: If any of us claim to be sinless, we are self-deceived and strangers to the truth.

P: Create in me a clean heart, O God, and put a new spirit within me.

L: We confess to attitudes that have resisted our growing

old and assumed that youth is better than age, ignoring the voices of wisdom and electing to follow paths of inexperience.

P: Create in me a clean heart, O God, and put a new spirit within me.

L: We lift up to you relationships that have become strained with time and friendships that have gone sour. Help us to heal what is broken and to find comfort in kinship that is good.

P: Create in me a clean heart, O God, and put a new spirit within me.

L: Heal memories that cause us pain, and help us to celebrate memories that bring us joy.

P: Create in me a clean heart, O God, and put a new spirit within me.

L: Forgive our dread of dying and our failure to hear your good news of salvation and eternal life.

P: Create in me a clean heart, O God, and put a new spirit within me.

L: We have been willing to go along with prejudice and warfare while hearing your challenges to peacemaking and love.

P: Create in me a clean heart, O God, and put a new spirit within me.

L: Almighty God: hear the prayers of your people; strengthen our lives with purpose and commitment, and help us to live as people who are forgiven.

ALL: Create in me a clean heart, O God, and put a new spirit within me.

Rev. Edward Loper, Clayville, New York
From *Agenda*. Used with permission.

Litany for Older Adult Week

L: God has promised, "Even to your old age and gray hairs I am he, I am he who will sustain you. I have made you and I will carry you." (Isa. 46:4 NIV)

P: We celebrate long life with God's promise to be close and to sustain us.

L: The role of the church is not to think of older adults in the context of frailty and vulnerability. This is a gifted generation, a generation blessed with experiences of a fast changing world. It is a generation filled with wisdom that comes from witnessing these great changes.

P: We celebrate the stability of God's people in this fast changing world and our feeling of belonging.

L: The role of the church is to awaken each of us to our gifts and talents. As Paul told Timothy, "I remind you to fan into flame the gift of God, which is in you . . . God did not give us a spirit of timidity, but a spirit of power, of love and of self discipline" (2 Tim. 1:6-7 NIV). All ages often feel that we have no talent. Lord, help us to recognize our talents and give us the willing spirit to use them.

P: We celebrate our gifts and talents, asking to be led to where these talents may be used in God's service.

L: The role of the church is to be venturesome. Let there be joy as we grow older and look for avenues of involvement, committing ourselves to the programs of the church and community.

P: Lord, help us to bubble with joy as we seek your guidance in finding new tasks to fill the hours of freedom that come with aging, discovering that old age can be full and satisfying.

L: The role of the church is to keep loneliness from creeping into older adult life. Let us keep in our hearts the passage "Because God has said, 'Never will I leave you; never will I forsake you' " (Heb. 13:5 NIV). The role of the church is to care and provide for the elders of the church family. "If any-one does not provide for his relatives . . . he has denied the faith and is worse than an unbeliever" (1 Tim. 5:8 NIV).

P: We celebrate our church family, the care and compas-sion of our congregation.

L: The role of the church is to be supportive of older adults' yearning to relate. We all need a mission, a purpose. We have contributions to make. God chose the elders when he wanted to bring about significant changes: Abraham, Sarah, Elizabeth, Zechariah, Simeon, Anna, Moses, Caleb, and oth-ers. May we, as today's elders, meet God's challenges for change.

P: We celebrate God's purpose for each of us.

ALL: We celebrate the role of the church in our lives today. We pray for God's help as we continually grow in faith, drawing strength from his Word. We support, console, encour-age, and love each other. May we meet the challenge of life as we grow closer to the graying years. Let us celebrate the gray hairs!

Carlita Hunter
From *Agenda*
Used with permission.

A Litany for the Church and Older Adults

L: You have called us to be the "light of the world and the salt of the earth."

P: Yet too often we have kept the light under a bushel and salted only our own food.

ALL: Forgive us, Lord.

L: You have commissioned your church to "feed my lambs, tend my sheep, and feed my sheep."

P: Yet we become preoccupied with programs, sabotaged by statistics, and swamped by a paralysis from analysis.

ALL: Forgive us, Lord.

L: In our church are many of God's older persons, some vibrant with energy, others victimized by disability.

P: Yet we continue to try to force them into old structures or view them with ageist eyes.

ALL: Forgive us, Lord.

L: Open our eyes, Lord, to how your church can serve older persons in society. Give us a new vision of Shepherd's Centers, elder care, sharing faith stories in groups, and advocates for nursing homes.

P: Yes, Lord, we are ready to go beyond the playpens for the elderly and the tea parties for the old. We want to take your church into new services for your wisdom people.

ALL: Let the words of our mouths and the meditation of our hearts be acceptable in your sight, oh Lord, our Strength and Redeemer.

Caleb Gerant

From *Agenda,* a free publication from the Presbyterian Church, U.S.A. To order write:

Agenda
Presbyterian Church USA
Room 5614
100 Witherspoon Street
Louisville, KY 40202-1396

New Texts for Familiar Tunes

"Create Us New"
Sung to the tune THE WATER IS WIDE

We lift our hearts, we bring our lives,

Just as we are, without disguise,
O Spirit come, create us new,
That we may walk in peace with you.

O holy flame of God that burns
Within each heart and truly yearns
To claim each heart, and make it new,
That we may love ourselves in you.

O holy wind, now sow your seed,
Let new life grow to noble deed,
O Spirit come, create us new
That we may serve this world for you.

Text: Rodney R. Romney. Words copyright © 1990
 AmaDeus Group. Used by permission.

"Come People, Gather and Rejoice"
Sung to the tune AZMON

Come people gather and rejoice, with all creation sing,
Join in the music of the spheres and let your voices ring.

We leave behind our daily cares to answer God's high call.
We come again to seek God's will and learn God reigns in all.

Our God is closer than our breath, in loving Presence near,
O hear the still, small voice within, "My loved one, I am here."

We offer up ourselves this day as channels of God's peace.
Thy Kingdom come, God's will be done, God's reign on earth
 increase.

Text: Barbara Neighbors Deal. Words copyright © 1990
 AmaDeus Group. Used by permission.

"Through All the Years"
Sung to the tune ALL SAINTS NEW

Through all the years, through countless days,
In those who led the way
We see the shining light of Love and courage to obey.
We see the steadfast faith and joy,
In them the promise made
To worship God, proclaim the Christ,
With courage to obey.

In times of pain, in times of doubt,
In days of dark despair
They called upon the living Christ
For courage all to bear.
They looked beyond the deepest grief
To pray the holy prayer;
"Thy Kingdom come, Thy will be done,"
With courage all to bear.

O may we live the nobler life
And follow in the way
Of valiant ones whose hearts were blessed
With courage day by day.
Inspire us with Divine Intent
And love, dear God, we pray,
That we may do thy will on earth
With courage day by day.

Text: G. Jean Anderson. Words copyright © 1990
   AmaDeus Group. Used by permission.

Note: For information on music by AmaDeus Group or for information on purchasing the book *Awaken Your Heart,* please write to:

> AmaDeus Group Publishers
> Route 1 Box 241
> Walla Walla, WA 99362

"For All the Joys of Living"
Sung to the tune LLANGLOFFAN

For all the joys of living
We thank thee, Lord, today
For childhood, youth, and later years,
For blessings on the way.
We come, O Lord, to praise thee,
The Source of all our dreams;
Not fear to walk, in older years,
The way where hope still gleams.

We thank thee, Lord, for wisdom,
Gained from our passing years;
A storehouse filled with memories,
The gift of joys and tears;
For visions that still beckon
Our footsteps on the way
Of service that will bless the world:
Give us new strength, we pray.

Let not the fear of aging
Consume our future days;
Give us the daily courage Lord,
To serve the untried ways.
Keep us from weak complaining,

Of years that now are gone;
May insights gained each passing year
Be light to lead us on.

Text: H. Glen Lanier. Copyright © 1976 by the Hymn
    Society of the U.S. and Canada. Used by permission.

"Come, Ye Elders, Those Engaging"
Sung to the tune CWM RHONDDA

Come, ye elders, those engaging
In the art of growing old;
Let us celebrate our aging,
Let our gratitude be told.

God, we praise thee; Lord, we thank thee,
For thy blessing manifold.

Nature still her bounty showers
For our pleasure every day;
Sunlight, moon-glow, rain and flowers,
Creatures small and children gay.

God, we praise thee; Lord, we thank thee;
Ever gratefully we pray.

Loving friendships long enduring
Sweeten hours with gracious thought.
Others, with their tender caring,
Comfort, peace and joy have brought.

God, we praise thee; Lord, we thank thee;
for thy grace bestowed unsought.

Time we have, at last, for dreaming;
Time to study; time to grow;
Latent talents thus revealing,
Richer lives we learn to know.

God, we praise thee; Lord, we thank thee
for the gifts thou dost bestow.

Aging is a time for gladness;
Fears and doubts let us destroy;
Let no heart be filled with sadness;
Celebrate! Glad songs employ.

God, we praise thee; Lord, we thank thee.
Fill our hearts with love and joy!

Text: Genevieve Lexow. Copyright © 1976 by the Hymn
Society of U.S. and Canada. Used by permission.

Note: For information on the pamphlet *10 New Hymns on
Aging and the Later Years,* write to:

> The Hymn Society in the U.S. and Canada
> National Headquarters
> Ed Landreth Hall, 2900 S. University Drive
> Fort Worth, TX 76129

Bibliography

Books

Becker, Arthur H. *Ministry with Older Persons: A Guide for Clergy and Congregations.* Minneapolis: Augsburg Fortress, 1986.

Bianchi, Eugene. *Aging As a Spiritual Journey.* New York: Crossroad, 1984.

Center for Learning. *Aging and the Parish Community: Workbook for Workshops.* Villa Maria, Pa.: Center for Learning, 1990.

Fischer, Kathleen. *Winter Grace: Spirituality for Later Years.* New York: Paulist Press, 1985.

Gentzlerr, Richard H., Jr. *Designing a Ministry By, With, and For Older Adults.* Nashville, Tenn.: Board of Discipleship, Section on Christian Education, P.O. Box 840, 37202-0840

Hunter, Carlita. *Grey Hair and I Don't Care: Leading Activities with Older Adults.* Atlanta, Ga.: Hunter House, 1984.

Kemper, Kristen. *Golden Opportunities: Older Adults and the Church.* Brea, Calif.: Educational Ministries, 1988.

Maitland, David. *Aging: A Time for New Learning.* Louisville, Ky.: Westminster/John Knox Press, 1987.

Sapp, Stephen. *Light on a Gray Area: American Public Policy on Aging.* Nashville, Tenn.: Abingdon, 1992.

Taylor, Blaine. *The Church's Ministry with Older Adults.* Nashville, Tenn.: Abingdon Press, 1984.

Vogel, Linda Jane. *Teaching Older Adults.* Nashville, Tenn.: Discipleship Resources, 1989.